089552

D1625865

Dior

First published in Great Britain in 1996 by
Thames and Hudson Ltd, London

Copyright © 1996 Editions Assouline, Paris

British Library Cataloguing-in-Publication Data
A catalogue record for this book is available from the British Library
ISBN 0-500-01721-2

Printed and bound in Italy

Dior

TEXT BY MARIE-FRANCE POCHNA

THAMES AND HUDSON

Fashion is an expression of faith. In this world of ours, that seeks to give away its secrets one by one, that feeds on false confidences and fabricated revelations, it is the very incarnation of mystery, and the best proof of the spell it casts is that, now more than ever, it is the topic on everyone's lips.

(*Christian Dior et moi* by Christian Dior,
Librairie Amiot, Dumont, 1956)

a swirling skirt twenty metres in circumference, hat tipped over one eye, haughty bearing. No dream, when she first appeared on 12 February 1947, but femininity incarnate, flirtatious, voluptuous, a blend of the outrageous and the elegant: a true Parisian allegory. This was the New Look, fifty years ago, the masterstroke that won back for Parisian couture the place it had lost during the war. Even now, many years later, the name Dior has lost none of its lustre. Though other masters of couture may be synonymous with a particular style, Dior expresses all the magic of fashion, its ability always to start afresh. It was Dior who brought about that marriage of the modern and the miraculous by transforming the role of haute couture. Until then, this was confined to a privileged minority; thanks to him it became the means of fulfilling the dreams of millions of women. 'Women, with their sure instincts, realized that my intention was to make them not just more beautiful but also happier.' A businessman as well as poet, he made fashion responsible for expressing society's desires and showed it how to communicate universally, establishing the democratic course of its future development.

His was a unique destiny, which his friend Jean Cocteau foresaw in his name: 'that magic name made up of the name of god and gold' ['god'/'gold' = 'Dieu'/ 'or' = Di/or]. The pun conceals a flattering reference by the Surrealist poet to the 'golden fortunes' that would be Dior's lot. For fifty years that name has been synonymous with luxury and high fashion. It has held its own against every other label, and now stands for a sort of perfection of discretion, elegance, femininity, and taste. Where did it come from? What is its essence? Why does it continue to inspire the designers of today? To find the answers, we must look at the life and work of Christian Dior. In everything he did, Dior was a true artist, although his progress was far from smooth: fate, accident and luck all played their part.

there was absolutely nothing to indicate that Christian Dior would make a career in fashion. Rather the reverse – which may explain the importance he accorded all his life to cards, astrology, clairvoyance, throws of the dice. He was born on 21 January 1905 in Granville, a Channel port that had lost its importance as a fishing centre and was now an elegant bathing resort. The family represented the very best of the solid bourgeoisie of the day: his uncle, Lucien Dior, was a minister; his father, Maurice Dior, grew ever richer as his fertilizer business prospered, and his elegant mother, Madeleine, made it her business to spend their wealth on making life as agreeable as possible. The future of the young Christian Dior appeared well mapped out. He was the second of a family of five children, reared on sound principles and surrounded by nannies. But in some ways he was unusual. He soon showed a genuine curiosity about the plants and flowers growing in the garden that Madame Dior created in Granville, and which became her masterpiece. And above all, it was clear that he had a precocious gift for drawing, which he demonstrated at carnival time. Granville was famous for its carnival, and the young Christian, carried away by the flower-decked floats and processions, excelled in devising fancy dress costumes. What might seem merely a childish game can now, in hindsight, be seen as a sign of real artistic gifts. But no one close to him was anxious to encourage leanings that did not correspond at all to their notions of a respectable career for a young man of standing. And when Christian Dior announced after his *baccalauréat* that he wanted to go to art school, he met with a firm refusal. It was the first real confrontation, but amicable, for Dior belonged to a generation that accepted the need to compromise with parental wishes. He agreed to enrol at the École des Sciences Politiques in Paris (his mother longed to have an ambassador for a son), but made no promises that he would not play truant.

dior was drawn to the lively bohemian side of Paris life: it was here, as it would turn out, that he would receive his true education. It was the time of the Boeuf sur le Toit, the Ballets Russes, exhibitions of abstract art, places where an elegant public mingled with the artistic community dominated by Jean Cocteau. Dior became part of a small group of talented young tearaways, future luminaries all: painters like Christian Bérard, musicians like Henri Sauguet and Les Six, writers like Maurice Sachs. Dior himself studied music, learned about painting, flirted with the avant-garde. In the end he failed his political science exams and his dilettante existence was threatened. His father, however, had tired of the fight and, faced with his son's passive resistance, agreed to put up the funds to open an art gallery. Christian's happiness was shortlived. In 1931, a series of bad investments swallowed up his father's entire fortune. There was a second confrontation, this time more acrimonious. The days of gilded youth were over: the time had come for Dior to earn his living.

It may not have seemed so at the time, but this cruel blow of fate was the means by which Christian Dior eventually came into his own. Granted, he lived through some dark years in the meantime, scouring the small ads for jobs, and as we would say today, 'of no fixed address' – which meant staying with friends and doing a moonlight flit, eating every second day, and winding up with tuberculosis. But at the end of it all, he was to recover the abilities he had let slip. One day, when he was in the depths of despondency after failing to get any of a number of jobs, a friend working in couture suggested he try sketching some designs. When they found favour, Dior applied himself further and took lessons, but his drawings already possessed a strange ability to capture life and movement, so that you could almost imagine the woman wearing the garment. After selling his designs all over the place for two years, he was taken on as a designer by Piguet. At that moment came the outbreak of the Second World War. This was a new trial to bear, though he was not the only one. Dior sought safety with his family in Callian, in the Var. When he returned to Paris, he found that his old job with Piguet had been filled, but was taken on by Lucien Lelong. There, gradually, the creative artist blossomed, and he began to chafe at playing a subordinate role. Dior was forty. When he looked around him, he saw all his friends were successes. Bérard was the toast of Parisian high society, and Pierre Balmain, his fellow disciple at Lelong, had just made a splash by launching his own couture house. It was high time to leave the nest.

After so many years of false starts and tentative beginnings (years when his talent was maturing and his true vocation emerging without his recognizing it), Dior's career suddenly took off. By chance he met the textile magnate, Marcel Broussac, one of the most powerful men in France, famous for his newspapers and his racing stable. Dior

7

knew how to be persuasive. At the end of the interview, and against all expectations, the cotton king declared himself willing to put up the money for Dior to open his own fashion house.

However difficult it may have been to imagine that a new fashion house, opening in the middle of a period of austerity and real poverty, could possibly rise to become number one in the whole world, the moment had come for Dior to follow his star. Had not the fortune-tellers he had consulted all his life assured him that success would come about through women? The twelfth of February was the fateful day when his fortunes were transformed. 'Yesterday unknown', wrote Françoise Giroud, 'Christian Dior became famous overnight.' The young editor of *Elle*, like all those attending the show, could hardly believe her eyes. How could anyone have the nerve to launch such a fashion? The first mannequin appeared, her whirling skirts sweeping away the dust of years. One, two, three models followed, echoing the first. Long skirts, narrow waists, full busts, it was unheard of... The women in the audience, in their short skirts and boxy jackets, began unconsciously tugging at their skirt hems. The day was won. And before long, the battle had spread to the streets.

What madness had made Dior do it? How could he dare preach luxury to a country paralysed by strikes — a quarter of a million strikers in Paris and three million in the country overall — where governments were collapsing and there were shortages of petrol, coal and fuel, and where just about everything else was unobtainable? In such circumstances, to introduce a fashion like this seemed a provocation. The reaction was not slow in coming. The newsreels showed astonishing scenes of women fighting in the street. What had happened was that housewives in the market at the Rue Lepic in the sixteenth arrondissement, still dressed like paupers, had lost their tempers at the sight of the first New Look frocks, launched themselves at their wearers, and actually beaten them up. The unfortunate victims were left half-naked. A most curious baptism of fire for haute couture. It had never previously expected to be worn in the street – and then along came Christian Dior, and suddenly it was a *fait accompli*. Soon women everywhere were rushing to buy material. The new fashion was the symbol of a return to happier times. Politics had no images to combat the general gloom, but the New Look channelled the desire of forty million French people to hold their heads high again, to be restored to the pleasures of life, love and good health. Dior was the first to be taken by surprise. All he had done was follow his hunch: 'If you are sincere and natural, the real revolutions take place without your trying.'

try or not, he succeeded in jumping an even more formidable hurdle: the Atlantic. America was to be crucial in the development of the New Look, even providing it with its name. Christian Dior had called his first collection 'Corolle', but the redoubtable Carmel Snow, editor-in-chief of *Harper's Bazaar*, rushed to be the first to congratulate the couturier with the words: 'It's quite a revolution, dear Christian. Your dresses have such a new look.' The news reached New York that day. Seventh Avenue (where the fashion industry was based), having been cut off from Europe during the war, had developed independently of Parisian couture. Yet in no more than a few months it was to fall into line. At a time when Europe had relinquished its leading role in the world, the American forces of liberation remained on European soil. The climate was right for something of a love affair to develop between the GIs and Gay Paree, which they passed through all too briefly on their way home. This infatuation had not a little to do with the speed with which the New Look took hold, bringing a touch of colour and glamour to the land of Uncle Sam, where even the Lucky Strike cigarette packets had turned khaki.

art of the New Look's strange dream-like power was the way the Americans thought they were recongnizing themselves in a set of images that was actually a return to the past. Dior's true genius lay in daring to move the goalposts. Not only did the New Look put an end to the ugliness of the wartime fashion of short skirts, padded shoulders, platform soles and cauliflower hats (what women did not put on their plates, they put on their heads), Dior also broke with the heritage of pre-war haute couture, a movement which, having absorbed the modernism of the twenties, was developing in the direction of an increased simplification and functionalism. Gabrielle Chanel was influential, with her masculine-style suits, in introducing a minimalist form of elegance. Dior rejected all of that, seeking his inspiration in the more distant past. Plunging décolletés, wide-brimmed hats tipped over one eye, rustling skirts, it is the Belle Époque that shines through, images of the past in the misty colours of Watteau or Winterhalter.

Should we therefore call Dior a reactionary? Of course not. No, he was endowed with the profound sensibility, intuitive understanding and independence of vision that are the hallmark of the true artist. 'Having taste means having your own taste,' he said. People wanted to forget the horrors of war. And with that memory, out too would go Cubism, concrete, and the geometric lines and sharp angles that could only recall the bruises left by the totalitarian machine. Not permanently, of course, for fashions are constantly changing, and Picasso, Le Corbusier and Chanel were already waiting again in the wings. Mademoiselle Chanel, in fact, had sought safety in Switzerland, and was enraged by Dior's success. She did not return until 1954, when there had been time for the scars to heal, thanks to Dior's colour and warmth, grace and opulence. That same grace was apparent in the neo-Louis XVI decoration of his mansion in the Avenue Montaigne, so reminiscent of the *fin de siècle* setting of his childhood, with its woodwork of Trianon grey, small-panelled doors, parlour palms and oval-backed chairs. And the same opulence Dior permitted himself in his second collection, which established the dominance of the New Look over the rest of fashion. The star of the show, the dress called 'Diorama', was made of black wool, its skirt was forty metres in circumference and it was of an unsurpassed stylistic perfection.

Still today that dress remains an archetype, to which fashion returns at regular intervals when sated with everything else. The eternal return to the eternal feminine: waist, ankles, breasts, gracefulness and glamour, or in other words, the resurgence of desire for the one thing in life that does not change. Following his success, Dior was invited to the United States, and only one year later, in November 1948, he was to open Christian Dior–New York. That date was a landmark, showing just how far he had travelled in his spectacular career for, although not as dazzling an occasion as the invention of the New Look, it represents a crucial stage in his life, the moment when he moved from haute couture to marketing clothes under his own label. It was a crucial change, and it may be seen as the foundation of the whole of the future luxury goods industry, for it was in New York that Dior transformed a craft activity into a diversified empire capable of serving as a model for the whole profession.

the designer went to the United States at the invitation of Neiman Marcus, the well-known Texas store, to be presented with their design Oscar. Now he discovered that vast continent, which hailed him as a star. Like a child Dior was bowled over by the sheer ease of life in a country where even cleaning ladies went to work in a Chevrolet. But, European to the core, he could not help noticing the things that were lacking in this great consumer society: a taste for luxury and a feeling for elegance. Moreover, a fierce controversy accompanied him throughout his American tour, concerning the New Look. The American woman was not to be won over instantly by the new silhoutte. The publicity was, as it turned out, the very thing that was needed to ensure its success. Already Dior noticed more or less crude copies appearing in the store windows. This annoyed him considerably. There was, he declared, no question of Seventh Avenue being allowed to pirate French designs. He came up with a novel and far-sighted plan: 'What we are selling is ideas,' he announced. His New York subsidiary would produce models specially designed for the American market; the patterns would be sold to the stores, who would make them up according to strict instructions. In the first five years of the House of Dior's existence, half its takings came from the New World.

Thus were the foundations laid of a commercial empire with an organizational structure that was to be transplanted to Cuba, Mexico, Canada, Australia, England, etc. The perfume 'Miss Dior' was launched in 1947, followed by 'Diorama' and 'Diorissimo'. Later creations were 'Poison' in 1985, 'Dune' in 1991, and most recently, 'Dolce Vita' in 1995. He said around 1550: 'A perfume is a door opening on to a rediscovered world. That is why I chose to create perfumes – so that merely taking the stopper from the bottle will be enough to summon up the sight of all my dresses, and so that every woman I dress will leave behind her a wake of desires. Perfume is the indispensable complement to the female personality, it provides the finishing touch to a dress, it is the rose with which Lancret signed his canvases.' He was to grant the first licences for stockings and ties at the same time as for the perfumes.

a s it expanded inexorably, the great fashion house became within very few years a complex centre of creativity. For the first time French notions of elegance and taste, symbolized by a label, became the basis for a vast business network. It employed 1,700 people among 8 companies and 16 subsidiaries, disseminating the brandname over five continents, but still retaining a tight hold over all its various activities. Till then no one had heard words like 'registered trademark', 'standard contract', 'brand image' or 'style bible'. Boussac provided Dior with the administrative and financial support to put everything on a proper business footing. He gave him a talented administrator, Jacques Rouët, who was a tower of strength in this period of growth. But it was Dior himself who, for example, instituted the idea of asking licence-holders to pay a percentage as a form of royalty. Such success was not without its detractors. Jacques Fath and, later, Pierre Cardin, were to follow his example, but such a bold approach furrowed the brows of certain colleagues accustomed to managing their artistic heritage like a traditional family business. Was not the prestige of couture at stake? The authorities, once alerted, intervened to try to forbid Dior from issuing a licence to a German manufacturer of jewelry. Dior had to defend himself. He was convinced he had done no more than drag his *métier* out of its craft ghetto, and was quite content to be called a popularizer; he made public his opinion that 'the supremacy of French quality and of our creative talent' could provide a new source of economic activity, by commercializing a tradition of taste and elegance that was distinctively French. But the prophet is without honour in his own country. And when he approached the powers-that-be about devising and setting up a system of legal defence against copying, which was still a huge problem, the request fell on deaf ears. One reason is that the French like their couturiers to be couturiers and their industrialists to be industrialists. With his dual personality, of creative artist and manager, Dior disconcerted more than a few of his contemporaries.

t alented young designers flocked around Dior. Pierre Cardin cut suits for the first collection, Jean-Louis Scherrer learned his craft there, Frédéric Castet, later to design the furs, was given his own atelier at the age of twenty-four. Dior was careful about promoting his staff — another feature that shows how unusual he was in a profession where the masters jealously guarded their fame and generally took little care to groom their successors. The opposite was true at avenue Montaigne. When in 1955 the firm took on a certain Yves Saint Laurent, Dior noted his talent and was the first to encourage the design prodigy of his generation, even making him his heir apparent. It was much the same with Marc Bohan, whom Dior had noticed at Patou, and took on only shortly before his death. When that shocking event occurred in the autumn of 1957 — Dior died of a heart attack while at the height of his powers — the future was already assured. For Dior had from the outset run his fashion house on proper business lines and made plain his desire that his own knowhow should be translated into standard procedures. An academy of style and taste, avenue Montaigne took on large numbers of draughtsmen, having by now become more or less the creative laboratory of an empire controlling a whole network of licences. One person who came under the Dior umbrella in 1953 was the shoe designer Roger Vivier, already well known in the United States, who was given a window on the corner of avenue Montaigne and rue François Ier. Shoes, essential to complete the silhouette, formed part of a sophisticated ensemble, the new 'total look', which the couturier brought in when he added his own gloves, handbags and jewelry to the range. A pioneer in this too, Dior opened his Grande Boutique to sell accessories and gifts, along with everything else the empire of Dior had to offer; and he allowed free rein to the talent of his friend Réné Gruau, whose timeless sketches brilliantly illustrate the spirit of the Dior woman.

So it came about that, when Dior died in 1957, the mantle passed immediately to Yves Saint Laurent, whose 'Trapeze Line' received a rapturous reception. He was succeeded in 1960, when he left to do military service, by Marc Bohan, who achieved a perfect marriage of his own creativity with fidelity to the spirit of Christian Dior, until his departure in 1989; at that date, Gianfranco Ferré was appointed as artistic director by the chairman Bernard Arnault, who had taken over the management of the company. The Italian designer brilliantly pursued the task of translating the spirit of elegance and perfection incarnate in the gold letters of the company's name. For the quest for perfection was a central feature of this academy of haute couture, its educational methods outlined by Dior in his book *Christian Dior and I* as if to give them the force of holy writ. The various different stages followed in strict sequence as though they were part of a prescribed ritual, guiding the couturier and his team through a long and serious process, from the inspiration of the first sketch, to the interaction with the skill of the ateliers, and the trying-on sessions in which a dress passed through a series of metamorphoses before emerging in its final form. And all this artistry devoted to the production of a mere 1,500 items per year. The fact that today all that skill is placed at the service of probably no more than two thousand clients worldwide has altered not one jot of the immutable protocol. The average time spent on a dress is 100-150 hours. But the collection itself is merely the keystone of a whole empire of beauty, whose mission is to spread its artistic influence far and wide.

dior the designer has occasionally been criticized for doing too much, and that could certainly be said of Christian Dior the man, who was driven by a passionate need to excel himself. From 1947-57, he continually sought fresh inspiration within the constraints of a style, creating two new lines each year: 'Corolle', 'Envol', 'Ailée', 'Verticale', 'Oblique', 'Muguet', etc. Dramatic masterstrokes, all of them, for which the public waited with bated breath. They received write-ups in the top newspapers of the day. But from the Americans, who found it all a bit too intense, it earned Christian Dior the nickname of 'dictator'. What they objected to – rightly – was this abuse of power, which every season decreed a different length or a particular cut, creating an absolute furore about hemlines and a public outcry we could scarcely conceive of today. Whether it was a good or a bad thing depends on your point of view, but it was an age when the elegant woman had to change her outfit four times a day! After 1950, the silhouette softened. The waist was relaxed in 1954 with the 'H Line', and the sack dress created an uproar. None of which prevented Dior from being alone responsible for half the exports of French fashion to the United States. Above and beyond the passage of time and social change, certain things endured: an unsullied tradition of elegance, a magnificent precision of style, a specific architecture of the silhouette, whose eminently recognizable pedigree had descended intact from its source. 'The dress', said Christian Dior, 'is an ephemeral piece of architecture designed to enhance the proportions of the female body.' Any flirtation with or concession to the more fanciful elements in fashion was thereby prohibited.

Let us remember, it was Dior who made black a colour, and perfected the little black wool dress that moulded the female contours as sleekly as the bodywork of a car. The suits too, in which he excelled, were designed to fit like a second skin. He introduced into the wardrobes of beautiful women a number of distinctively masculine features, such as Prince of Wales and hound's-tooth checks, so creating codes of dress that – as so often with Dior – were to prove timeless. Another constant was his love of cloth that would hang well and had volume, allowing him to achieve the softly rounded drapery that was another of his specialities. For evening wear he created sumptous gowns, floating creations in tulle or organza, either printed or bearing motifs of embroidered flowers of rare beauty. All Christian Dior's effort went into the constant search to achieve a balance between discipline and softness, tradition and invention. Classic lines, with here and there a few tricks slipped in for shock value (his *coups de Trafalgar*, as he called them). Hence the impression of a panther bursting onto the fashion scene with an evening gown that takes everyone's breath away...

dior was also an inexhaustible source of refinements in garment construction, something to which the wonderful genius of the ateliers, which still today are the jewel of the world of couture, bears witness. As for the fantastic evening gowns, these too have come to symbolize the fairytale tradition that dates all the way back to the New Look and the birth of the House of Dior. The instant fame of that first collection acted as a catalyst for a revival in the arts of living, in a free world of which Paris became the centre. Those were the euphoric days of café society, that mixture of the cosmopolitan and the aristocracy of the Tout-Paris, who revived the tradition of elaborate parties and grand private balls. A Dior collection was an event as eagerly anticipated as the theatre hit of the season. In the designer's own mind, it was like a revival of a lost world, a celebration of the past, which you were drawn into by the beauty of the clothes, the wonder and magnificence of the production, the spectacle conjured up by the couturier, in which the dresses took the leading roles. Each was given its own name, and the subject of the 'play' was indicated by the collection's theme, which might reflect any one of the various worlds the couturier held dear: theatre, opera, literature, flowers, historic towns, Paris, and sometimes his private world of gambling, cards and mysteries.

At the opposite end of the spectrum from this theatrical taste lay the austere genius of Balenciaga, who refused even to greet the audience at the end of his shows; it was Dior's influence that won over the rest of Paris couture to this means of highlighting the presentation of their models. The glorious tradition continued at Avenue Montaigne and reached a pitch of splendour at the time of the 1995 Summer collection, in Gianfranco Ferré's tribute to Paul Cézanne.

By exercising his craft like a high priest, and raising haute couture to an apogee of perfection, Christian Dior imparted to his fashion house an atmosphere of taste, delight and elegance which guaranteed its future. Fifty years after its foundation, the name of Christian Dior has achieved the double distinction of being the only couturier quoted on the stock exchange and a company at the head of an empire that is the world's leading purveyor of luxury goods.

Yet behind this brilliant achievement was an affectionate, shy, funny and essentially solitary man, who remained wary of his fame and one day movingly declared: 'I have always regarded the exercise of my profession as a struggle against everything in our age that is mediocre and depressing.' For the heirs of Christian Dior, that statement has acquired an inspirational force, giving the House of Dior the dynamic impetus that carries it successfully through the passing years.

LA LIGNE DIABOLO

Les Gants Christian Dior

Christian Dior

Souliers créés par

Roger Vivier

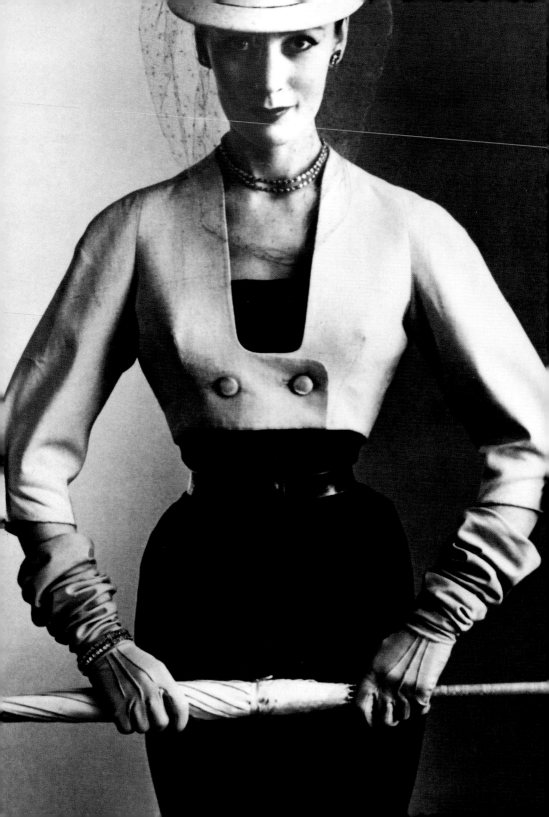

TWENTY CENTS

MARCH 4, 1957

TIME

THE WEEKLY NEWSMAGAZINE

CHRISTIAN DIOR

$6.00 A YEAR

VOL. LXIX NO. 9

224
Lucky

225
Odile

Fourreau de
velours noir. Manches
très collantes et dé
profond.
large ceinture de sa
blanc drapé placée
au dessus de la tail
normale

y. Mathieu Saint Laurent
55.

Monique

19 JUIN 1950

Christian DIOR
30, Avenue Montaigne-PARIS-8e
Croquis No 166

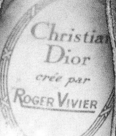

Chronology

1946 Opening of the fashion house Christian Dior, on 16 December, in a small private mansion at 30, avenue Montaigne.

1947 Presentation of the first collection, Spring-Summer 1947. The lines 'Corolle' and '8' stun the fashion world.
Dior receives a fashion award from Neiman Marcus in Dallas (USA).
Creation of the perfume christened 'Miss Dior' in tribute to Dior's sister, Catherine.

1948 Opening of Christian Dior–New York and Christian Dior Perfumes–New York.
Christian Dior Furs opens in Paris.

1949 Dior is the first couturier to license his products.
Launch of the perfume 'Diorama'.
At the 'Milieu du siècle' collection, Autumn-Winter 1949-1950, more than 1,200 orders for dresses are placed in one week.

1951 Opening of Christian Dior Stockings and Gloves, with 900 staff.

1953 Opening of Christian Dior Delman S.A.R.L., manufacturing made-to-measure shoes designed by Roger Vivier.
Frédéric Castet becomes head of the tailoring atelier.
The line 'Vivante', in the collection Autumn-Winter 1953-1954, is baptized the 'Shock Look' in England because the skirts are shortened to 40 centimetres off the ground.
Creation of 'Eau Fraîche'.

1954 Opening of Christian Dior Ltd, Dior's first London shop.
In Paris, the House of Dior employs a staff of 1,000, occupies 5 buildings with 28 ateliers and accounts for more than half of all French haute couture fashion exports.
The 'H Line', in the collection Autumn-Winter 1954-1955, is nicknamed the 'French Bean' Line or 'Flat Look'.

1955 Opening of the Grande Boutique on the corner of the avenue Montaigne and the rue François Ier.
Opening of the Gifts and Tableware Department.
Christian Dior lectures at the Sorbonne to 4,000 students.
Yves Saint Laurent is appointed to the design staff and becomes Dior's first and only assistant.
Launch by Christian Dior Perfumes of their first lipsticks.

1956 Creation of the perfume 'Diorissimo'.

1957 Christian Dior dies of a heart attack.
Yves Saint Laurent is appointed artistic director.

1958 YYves Saint Laurent shows the 'Trapeze Line' in his first collection, Spring Summer 1958.
Marc Bohan is appointed artistic director of Christian Dior, London.

1960 : Marc Bohan succède à Yves Saint Laurent comme directeur artistique à Paris.

1961 Marc Bohan presents his first Haute Couture collection, Spring-Summer 1961, the 'Slim Look'.
Liz Taylor orders twelve dresses.

1963 Creation of the perfume 'Diorling'.

1966 Creation of the first eau-de-toilette for men, 'Eau Sauvage'.

1967 First collection of women's ready-to-wear, 'Miss Dior', created by Philippe Guibourgé.
Introduction of the 'Baby Dior' line.
Marc Bohan designs the bridal and coronation gowns for the Empress Farah Diba, also those of her attendants.

1968 Frédéric Castet takes over the Haute Fourrure division.

1969 Launch of the first line of Christian Dior cosmetics.

1970 Launch of 'Christian Dior Monsieur', under Marc Bohan's direction.

1972 Creation of the perfume 'Diorella'.

1973 Launch of the *Prêt-à-Porter* fur collection by Frédéric Castet.
Launch of the beauty product 'Hydra-Dior'.

1979 Launch of the perfume 'Dioressence'.

1983 Marc Bohan is awarded the Dé d'Or for his Haute Couture collection, Spring-Summer 1983.
Dominique Morlotti succeeds Gérard Penneroux as designer for 'Christian Dior Monsieur'.

1984 Launch of the eau-de-toilette 'Eau Sauvage Extrême'.

1985 Bernard Arnault, chairman of the Agache Group, is appointed chairman and managing director of Christian Dior.
Launch of the perfume 'Poison'.

1986 Launch of the beauty product 'Capture'.

1987 To mark the fortieth anniversary of the House of Dior, a major retrospective is held at the Musée des Arts de la Mode: 'Hommage à Christian Dior 1947-1957'.

1988 A second Dé d'Or is awarded to Marc Bohan for his Haute Couture collection, Autumn-Winter 1988-1989.
Launch of the perfume 'Fahrenheit'.

1989 Gianfranco Ferré succeeds Marc Bohan and Frédéric Castet. 'Ascot-Cecil Beaton', his first Haute Couture collection, Autumn-Winter 1989-1990, wins the Dé d'Or.
Launch of the eau-de-cologne 'Poison' and the 'Icône' range of beauty products.

1991 Launch of the perfume 'Dune'.

1992 Patrick Lavoix is appointed artistic director of 'Christian Dior Monsieur'.

1994 A major retrospective entitled 'Christian Dior, the Magic of Fashion', tracing Christian Dior's ten years of design, is held at the Powerhouse Museum, Sydney, Australia.

1996 Fiftieth anniversary of the House of Dior.

Christian Dior

Drawing by René Gruau of the New Look silhouette: long skirt, narrow waist and full bust. Archives Christian Dior.
The famous 'Bar' suit, keynote model of the New Look collection, 12 February 1947. Photo: Ass. Willy Maywald. © ADAGP, Paris 1996. Archives Christian Dior.

Dior's bold panther print made its first appearance in the collection Spring/Summer 1947, in two versions: 'Afrique' for evening and (here) 'Jungle' for day. Photo: Bellini. Archives Christian Dior.
Advertisement for 'Miss Dior'. Drawing by René Gruau, 1949. The juxtaposition of a woman's hand and panther's paw refers both to Cocteau's film, based on *Beauty and the Beast,* and to Dior's first collection. Archives Christian Dior.

Cover of Match, August 1952. Dior's ironic smile anticipates the sensation it will cause when he decrees a skirt length of 40cms off the ground. © AFP. Archives Christian Dior.
The Dior silhouette, as interpreted by the talented illustrator Mats Gustafson for Gianfranco Ferré's Haute Couture Collection, Autumn/Winter 1989. © Photo: Mats Gustafson, A + C Anthology.

The ritual of the final rehearsal. Christian Dior and his team review the models for the Haute Couture Collection, Autumn/Winter 1954-1955. Photo: Walter Carone. © Scoop/Paris Match.

The same, but different. As the seasons change, so do the materials: draped crêpe and chiffon in the Haute Couture Collection, Spring/Summer 1953 (left), hangs quite differently when interpreted in fine wool in the Haute Couture Collection, Autumn/Winter 1953 (right). Archives Christian Dior.

Portrait of Christian Dior by Cecil Beaton in his private mansion at Boulevard Jules Sandeau. © Cecil Beaton Photography, Courtesy of Sotheby's, London.
A classic contrast. A simple white linen bolero relieves the full-skirted gown of draped black chiffon taffeta, in the model 'Meilhac', from the Haute Couture Collection, Spring/Summer 1952. Archives Christian Dior.

Advertisement for gloves, 1948. Drawing by René Gruau. Christian Dior allowed Gruau a free hand in producing his elegant, assured and irreverent illustrations of the Dior woman. Archives Christian Dior.

'Gascogne', Autumn/Winter 1950. For Dior, a dress was an 'ephemeral piece of architecure' designed to enhance the proportions of the female body. Archives Christian Dior.

The success of the collection meant squeezing close friends in on the stairs. Dior wrote: 'The clientèle I dreamed of responded to my call, I never had to make any particular effort.' Photo: Ass. Willy Maywald. © ADAGP, Paris 1996 (right); © Photo: All rights reserved. Archives Christian Dior (left).

Constructing a silhouette. The dresses would not exist at all without the patient work of the seamstresses. Photo: Bellini. Archives Christian Dior.

The line for Autumn/Winter 1954 is based on a full skirt and smaller bust, the slender grace of an adolescent or ballerina. Photo: Coffin. Archives Christian Dior.

Drawing by René Gruau advertising shoes designed by Roger Vivier at Christian Dior in 1960. Archives Christian Dior.

Dior's mannequins in 1957. Right to left, front: Simone, Sveltaka, Lucky, France. Second row: Olga, Catherine, Alla. On ladder: Renée and Victoire, whom Dior took on in spite of unanimous disapproval and made a star. Photo: L. Dean/*Life Magazine*/Time Warner Inc/Cosmos. Archives Christian Dior.

'Zémire': Autumn/Winter 1954. 'H Line'. Satin evening ensemble. Jacket with 'Lutetia' Emba mink trim. Photo: Regina Relang. © Münchner Stadtmuseum. Archives Christian Dior.

'Bleu de Perse'. Autumn/Winter 1955-1956. 'Y Line'. Dress and paletot in Persian blue tweed. Photo: Regina Relang. © Münchner Stadtmuseum. Archives Christian Dior.

The art of drapery. Detail of 'Moulin Rouge'. Haute Couture Collection, Autumn/Winter 1954-1955. Archives Christian Dior.

For Dior, the ideal mannequin was the one on whom 'any dress appeared successful, so closely did her proportions match the ideal of my dreams'. Photo: Bellini. Archives Christian Dior.

'Cachotier'. Haute Couture Collection, Spring/Summer 1951. 'Ovale' line. Dior superimposes three ovals: head; bust in ivory Shantung spencer; and hips, encased in anthracite grey alpaca. Photo: Poitier. © Bibliothèque Nationale de France, Paris. Archives Christian Dior.

Clean, elongated lines are the mark of this slender-fitting coat in satin-finish white wool. Haute Couture Collection Autumn/Winter 1957. Archives Christian Dior.

The Grande Boutique. Dior's distinctive neo-Louis XVI style, with its painted woodwork, white with Trianon grey, and oval-backed chairs. Photo: Laziz Hamani.

1957. The first couturier in the world to appear on the cover of *Time* magazine. © RAPHO. Archives Christian Dior.

Contemporary silhouettes. For lunch or dinner, 'Mystère de Paris', Haute Couture Collection, Autumn/Winter 1955-1956. Photo: Henry Clarke. © ADAGP, Paris 1996. Archives Christian Dior..

Roger Vivier's designs were shown with the main collection and sold made-to-measure in the boutique. For Dior in 1959, this high-heeled shoe in black suede with its 'shock' heel was the epitome of Parisian elegance. © Photo: Cynthia Hampton.

This design by Yves Saint Laurent, Dior's assistant, offers a foretaste of his talent: sketch (left) of 'Soirée de Paris' (shown right), Haute Couture Collection, Autumn/Winter 1955-1956. This black velvet sheath with fitted sleeves, low neck and wide draped belt in white satin represents a change of silhouette within the same overall style. Archives Christian Dior. © Photo: All rights reserved.

'Chantecler', Autumn/Winter 1954-1955. Two-piece suit in chiné brown tweed. In 1954, Dior abandoned the New Look, the waist was relaxed and the line softened. Archives Christian Dior. © Assouline.

'Balmoral', Haute Couture Collection, Autumn/Winter 1961-1962. Dress and jacket ensemble in Chaldean brown, Prince of Wales check wool, designed by Marc Bohan. Archives Christian Dior.

Christian Dior was the first to use distinctive stylistic features as his personal trademark: here, the neo-Louis XVI oval-backed chair, white boxes, monogrammed ribbon and houndstooth check. Archives Christian Dior. © Assouline.

Houndtooth court shoe. Dior's favourite motif is given a futuristic interpretation by Roger Vivier in 1959: pointed toe and 'Tibet' heel. © Photo: Cynthia Hampton.

'Braise', dress by Gianfranco Ferré, Haute Couture Collection, Autumn/Winter 1989-1990. Draped wrap in 'flame red' taffeta, trimmed with roses. Photo: Michael O'Connor. Archives Christian Dior.

'Ispahan', 1947 dress illustrated by René Gruau in the review *Adam*. The neckline of roses attracts admiration; pearls, gloves, stilettoes and Dior red complete the picture. Archives Christian Dior.

The Dior influence lives on. The redingote, a timeless favourite: in white shantung for Gianfranco Ferré's Prêt-à-Porter Collection, Spring/Summer 1991; and Dior's sketch for the Haute Couture Collection, Autumn/Winter 1950-1951. Archives Christian Dior (left); © Photo: Giovanni Gastel, Boué & Schack (right).

'Pisanelle'. Autumn/Winter 1949, 'Milieu de siècle'. Evening wear ensemble in midnight-blue satin and velvet, the full drapes suggestive of 15th/16th-century Venetian painting. Photo: Ass. Willy Maywald. © ADAGP, Paris. 1996.
'Lucie'. 'Images dans le miroir' Collection, Autumn/Winter 1993. Titian and Veronese provide the models for this dress in gold crushed panne velvet, worn by Italian actress Alba Clemente. © Michel Comte, *Vogue Italia*, 1994.

The perennial white blouse. Transparency and rhinestone buttons, Prêt-à-Porter Collection, Autumn/Winter 1993-1994. © Photo: Mikael Jansen. Archives Christian Dior.

The 'Verticale' Line, Spring/Summer 1950. Dior gives a flowing line to draperies, pleats and bustles. Photo: Ass. Willy Maywald. © ADAGP, Paris, 1996. Archives Christian Dior.
'Jardin aux Roses'. Spring/Summer 1992. Gianfranco Ferré's chiné, flower-printed taffeta has this same cascading effect. © Photo: Albert Watson, Elizabeth Watson Inc.

Carla Bruni in the dress 'Adalia', Haute Couture Collection, Spring/Summer 1995. Contrasting images and materials as the sweep of shantung is combined with frothy tulle. © Photo: Roxanne Lowit. Archives Christian Dior.

The splendours of Haute Couture. Bustier in embroidered gold brocade on a dress in Jacquard-weave crushed gold lamé: 'Rivière', Collection Autumn/Winter 1993-1994. Photo: Frédéric de Lafosse. Christian Dior Archives.
Dior loved accessories, and this shoe in printed silk by Roger Vivier shows the care lavished on accessories at the House of Dior: they 'made' an outfit. © Photo: Noelle Hoeppe.

The classic 'Bar' two-piece. Reinterpreted here by Gianfranco Ferré for the Prêt-à-Porter Collection, Spring/Summer 1996. Photo: Jeff Manzetti.
Dior style: the dresses look as good inside as out. Photo: Jeff Manzetti.

With 'Miss Dior' in 1947, Dior began a tradition of fine perfumes. Haute Couture, Autumn/Winter 1948. 'Dior's collection was awaited as eagerly as the opening of an opera...'(Helène Rochas)

Bibliography

Dior, Christian, *Christian Dior et moi*, Dumont Paris, 1956.
Published as, *Dior by Dior*, translated by Antonia Fraser,
Weiderfield and Nicolson, London, and Dutton, New York, 1957.
Giroud, Françoise, *Christian Dior*, photos: Sacha Van Dorrsen, Thames and
Hudson, London, 1987.
Keenan, Brigid, *Dior in Vogue*, Octopus Books, London 1981.
Pochna, Marie-France, *Christian Dior*, Éditions Flammarion, Paris, 1994.
'Hommage à Christian Dior', exhibition catalogue, Musée des Arts du
Costume, Paris, 1987.

The publishers wish to thank the Maison Christian Dior and Marika
Genty in particular for her invaluable assistance in producing this book.
Thanks are due also to: Roxanne Lowit, Michel Comte, Lucia Vietri,
Albert Watson, Elizabeth Watson, Mats Gustafson, Mimi Brown, Laziz
Hamani, Jeff Manzetti, Cynthia Hampton, Lydia Cresswell-Jones,
Sotheby's London, Giovanni Gastel, Corinna Shack, Mikael Jansen,
Sébastien Roca, Yannick Morisot, Alba Clemente, Nadège Dubospertus,
Fabienne Terwinghe, Eiser White, Carla Bruni, Véronique Jacqueti (FORD
Paris), Cathy Queen (FORD NY) and Sabine Killinger (ELITE).